LOOKING DOWN

LOOKING
DOWN

BY STEVE JENKINS

HOUGHTON MIFFLIN COMPANY
BOSTON NEW YORK

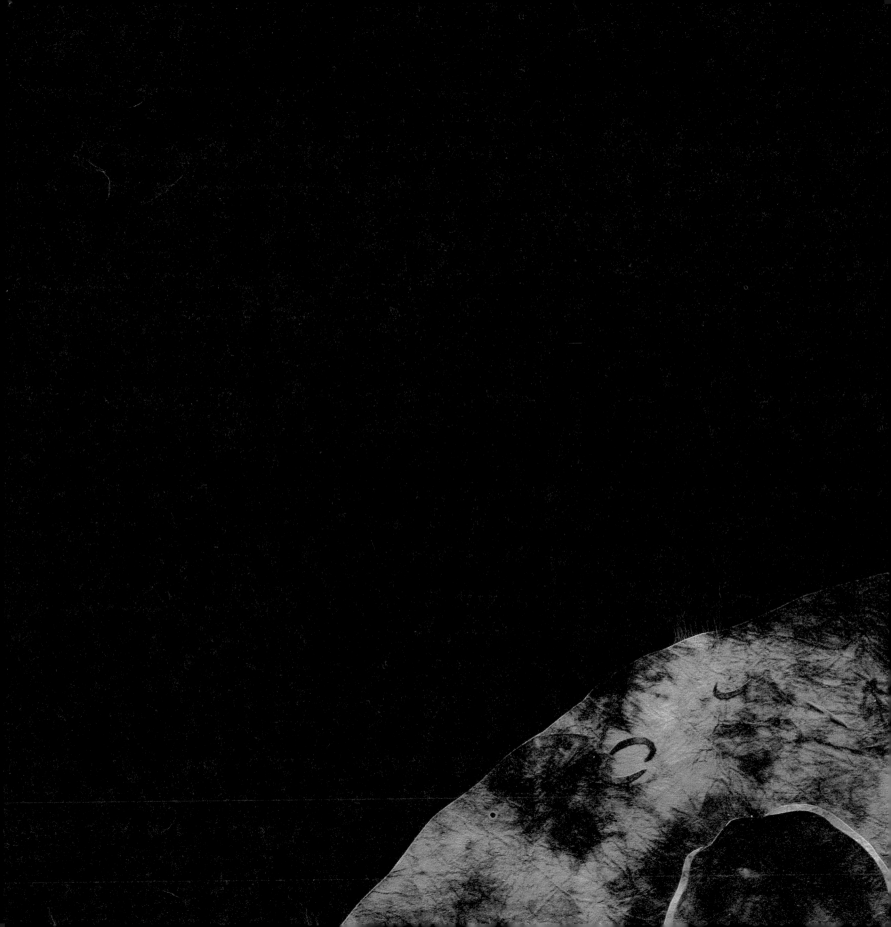

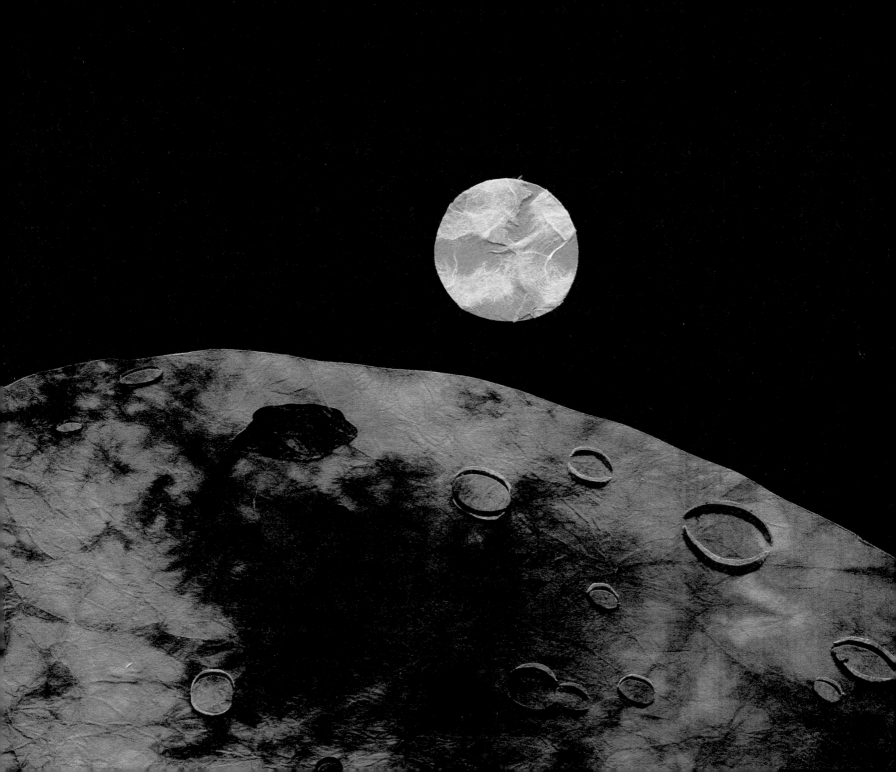

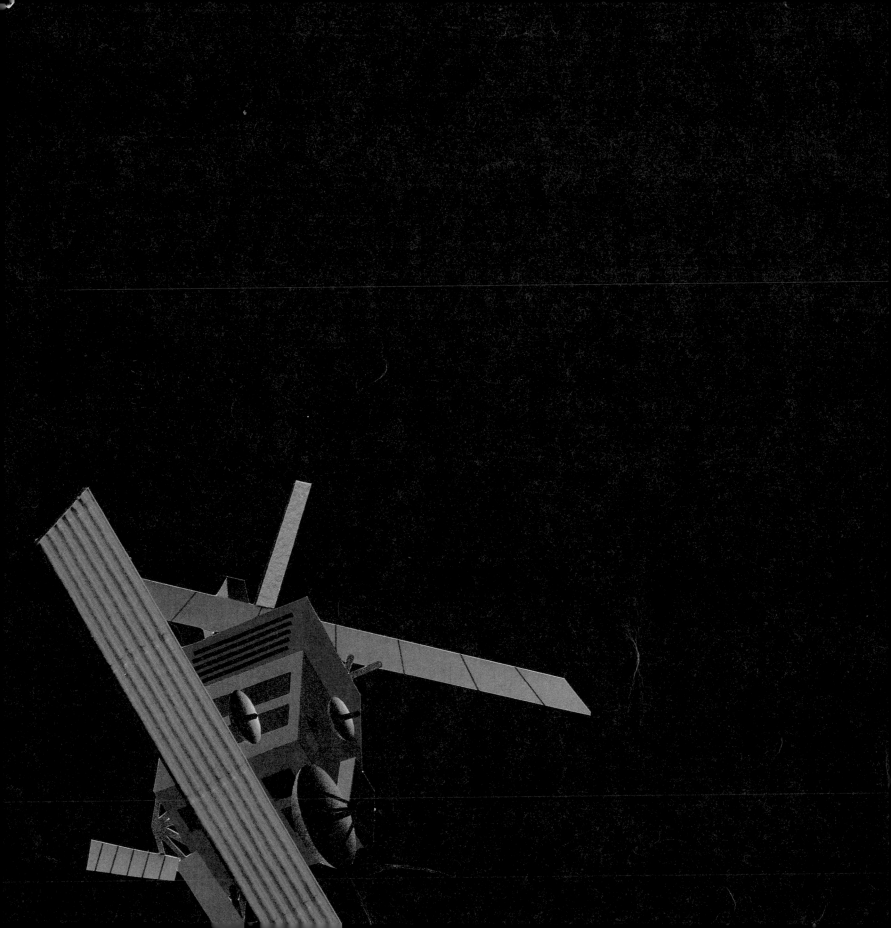

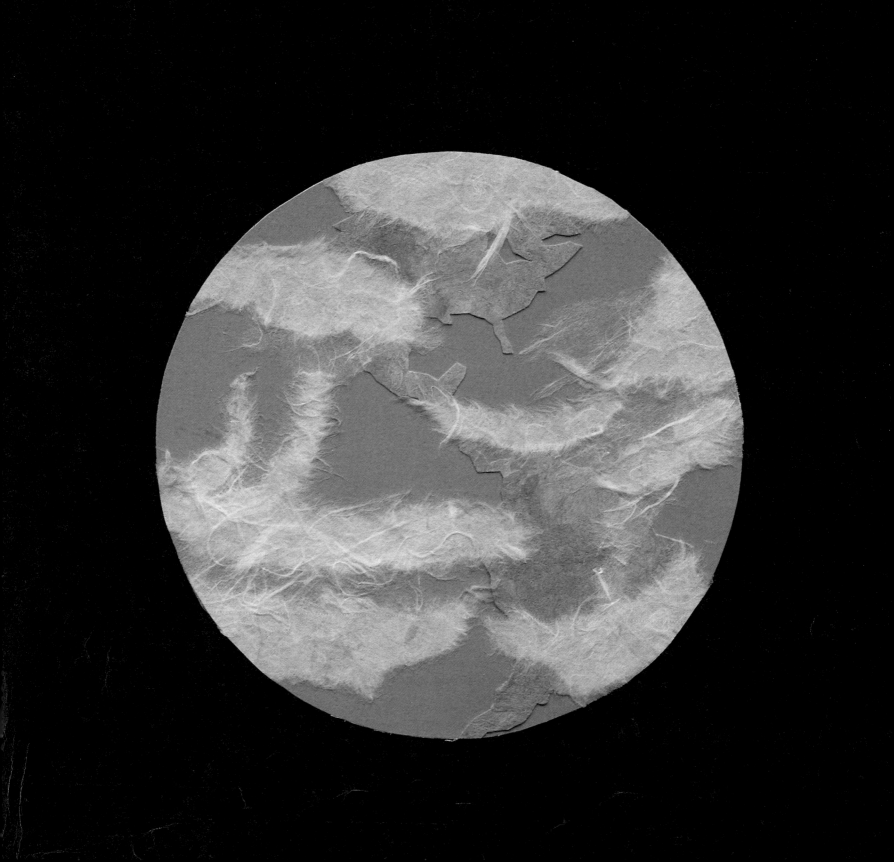

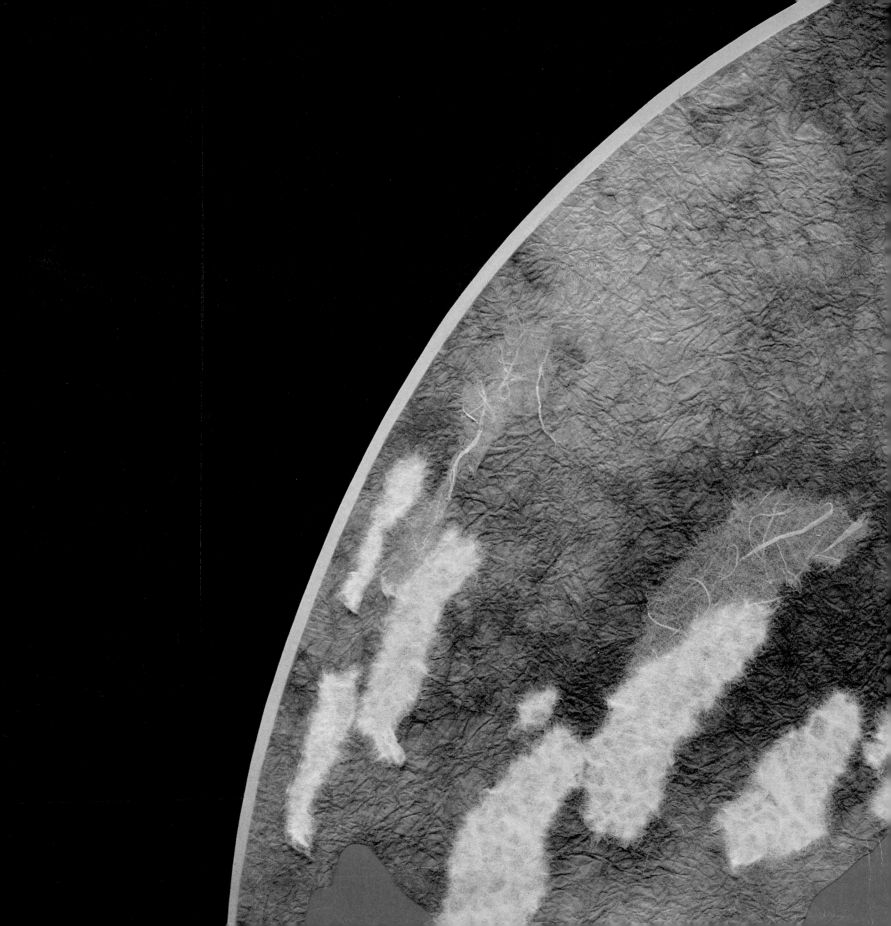

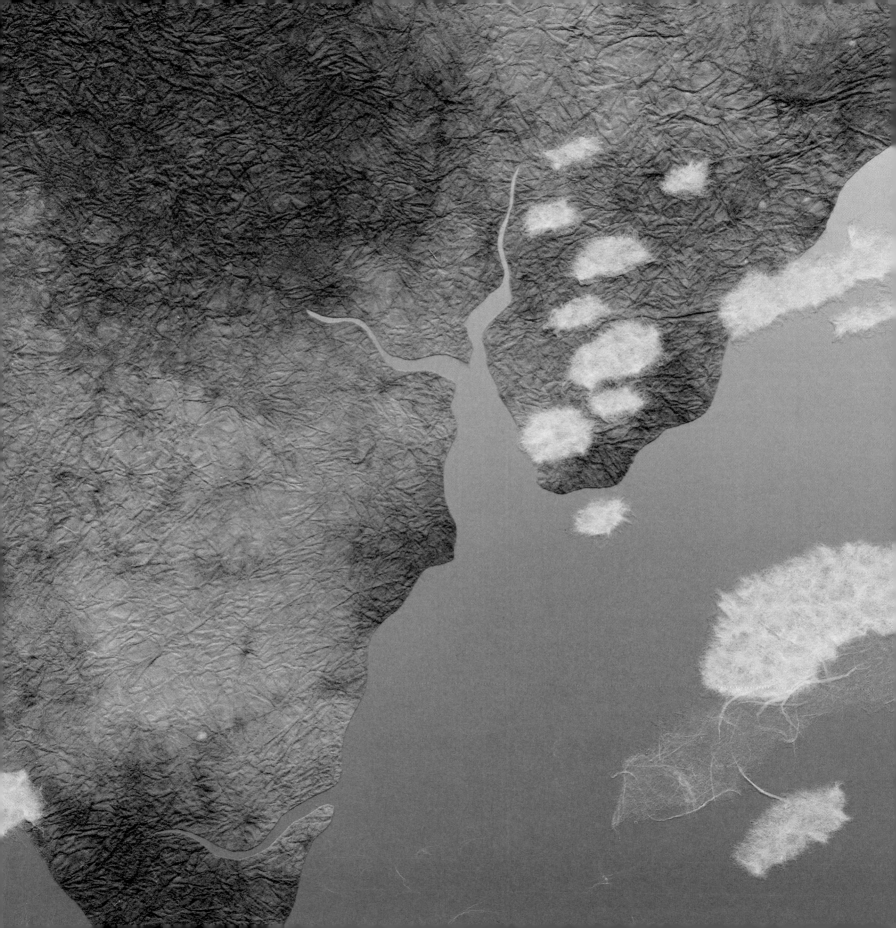

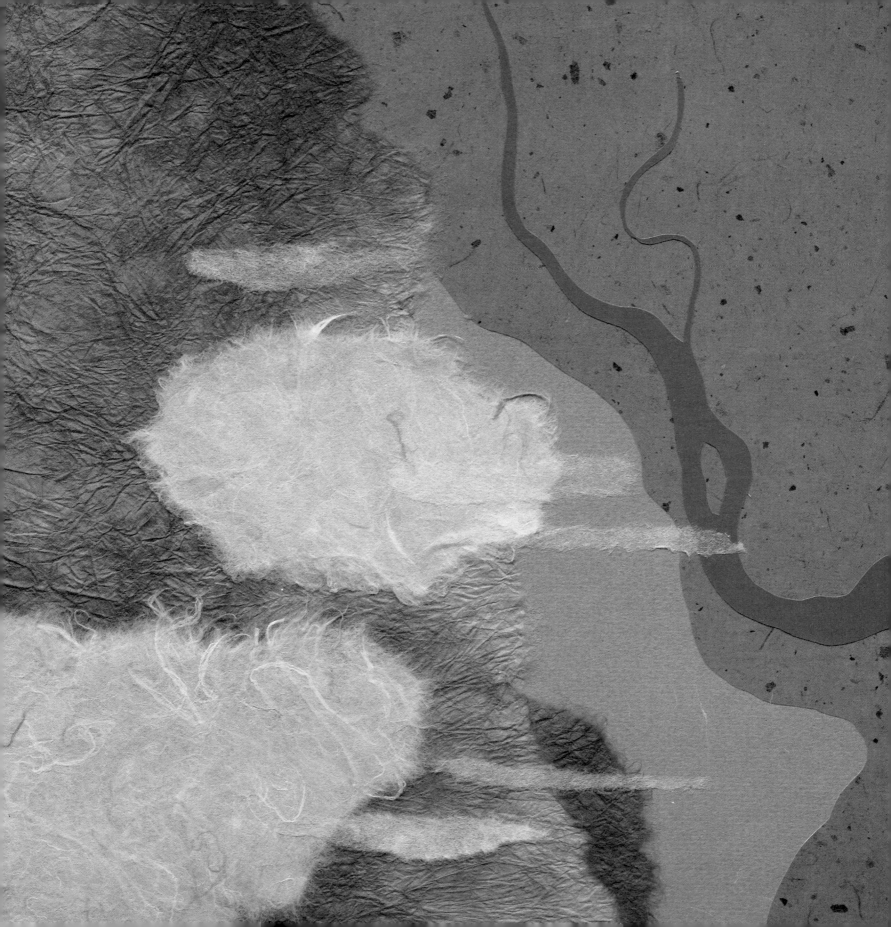

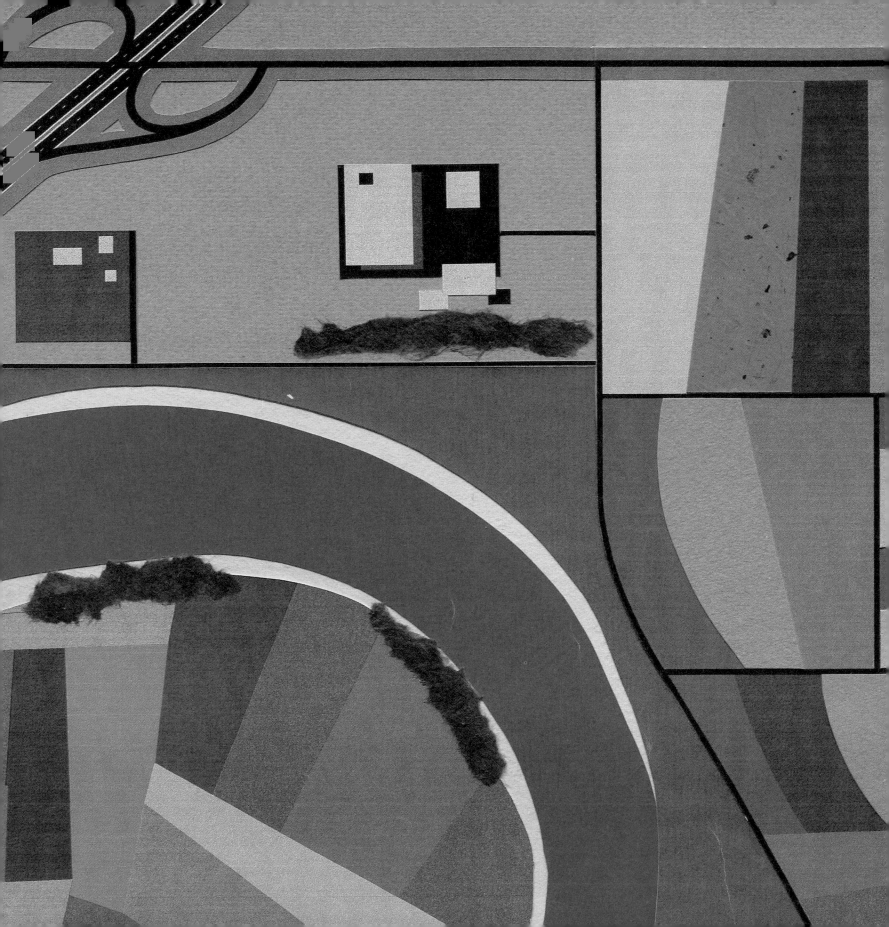

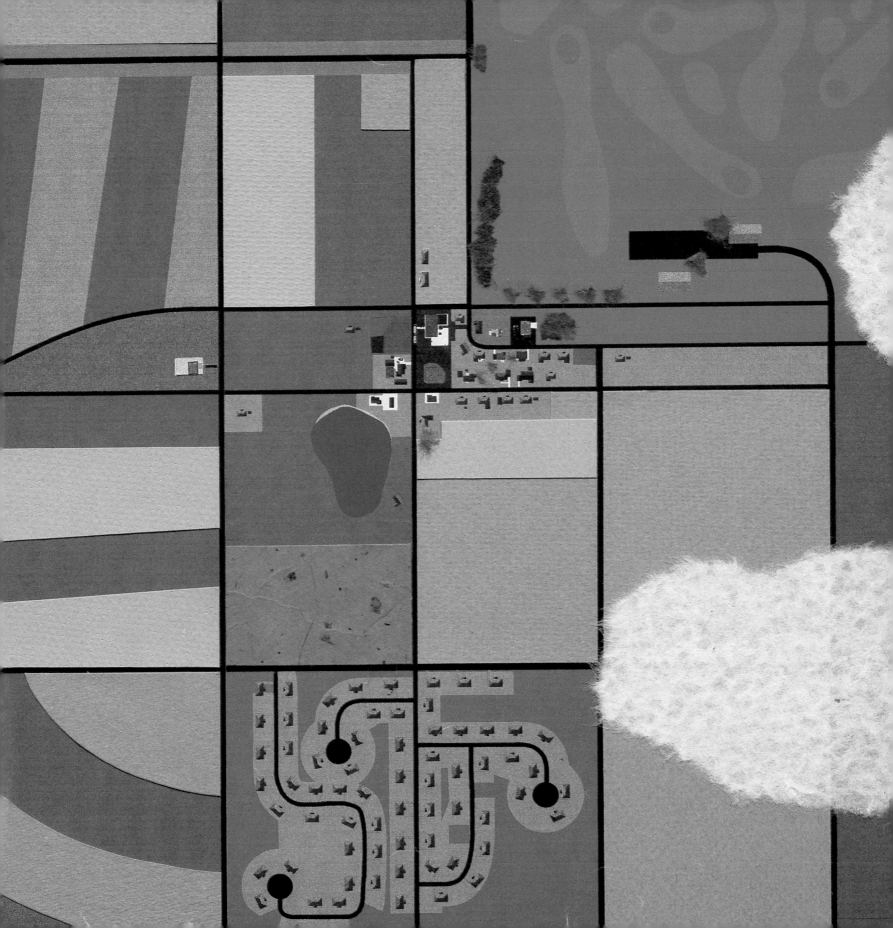

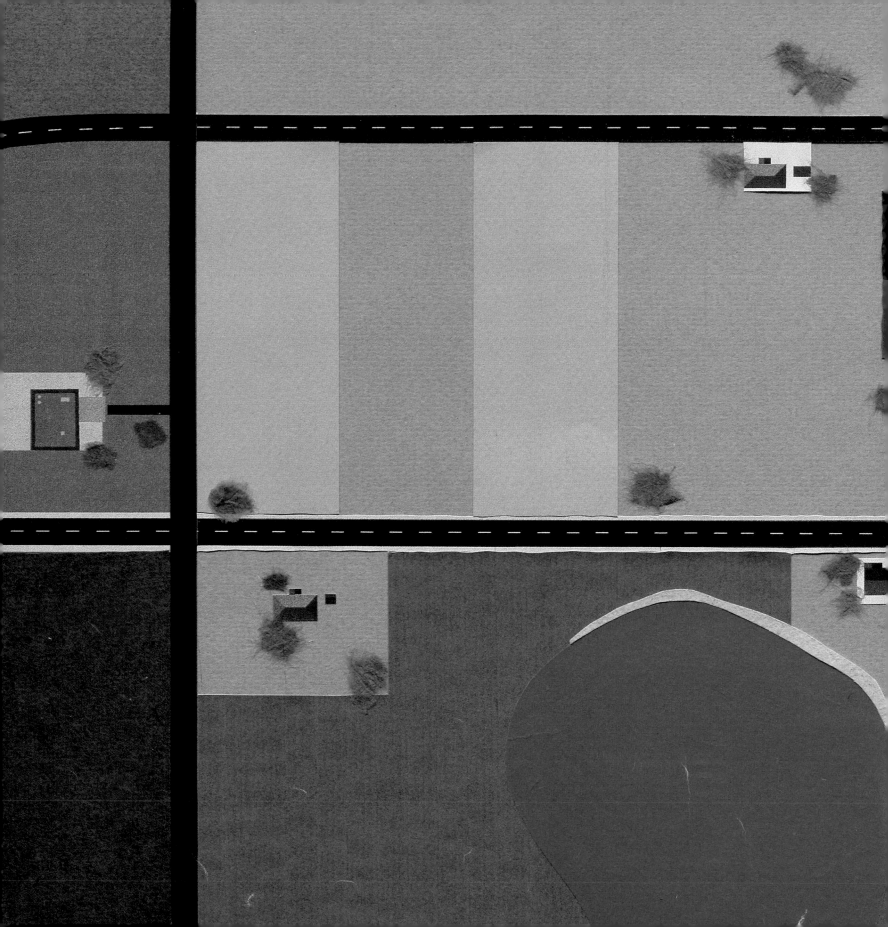

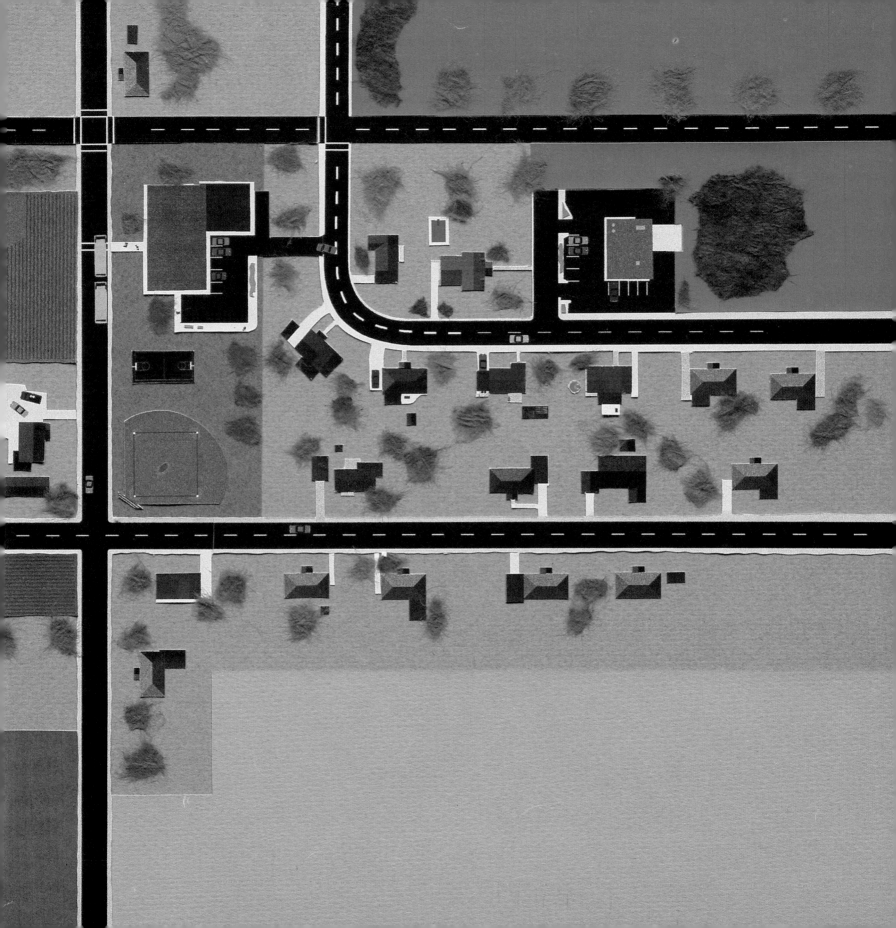

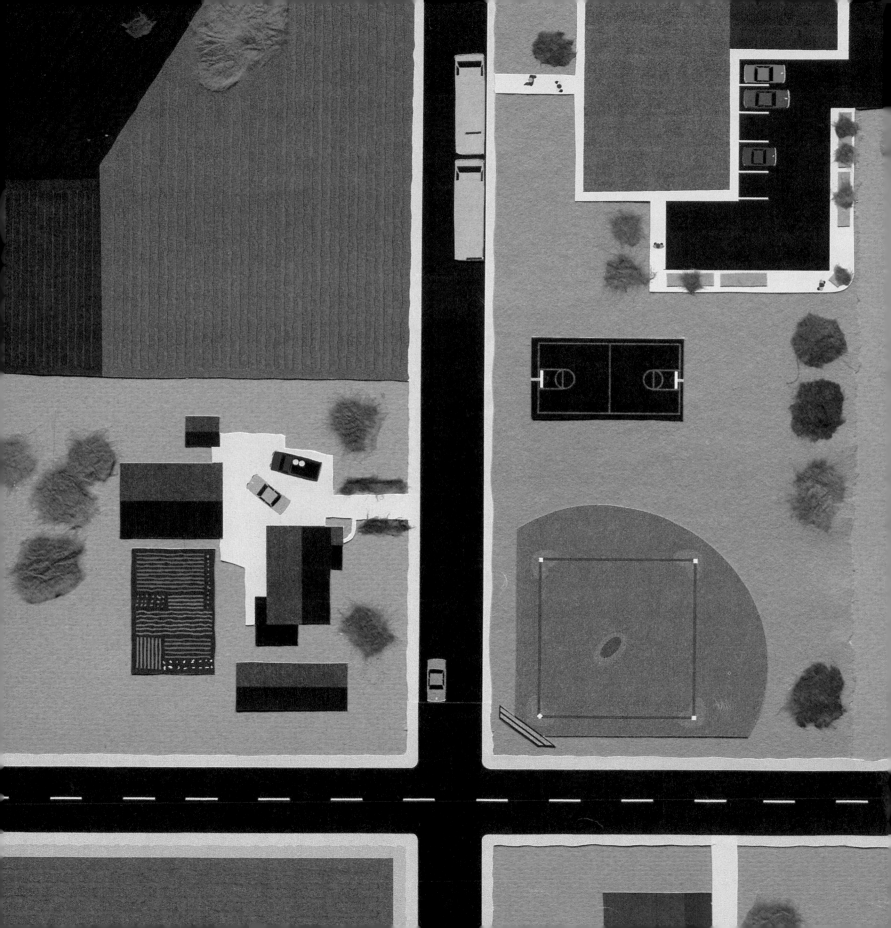

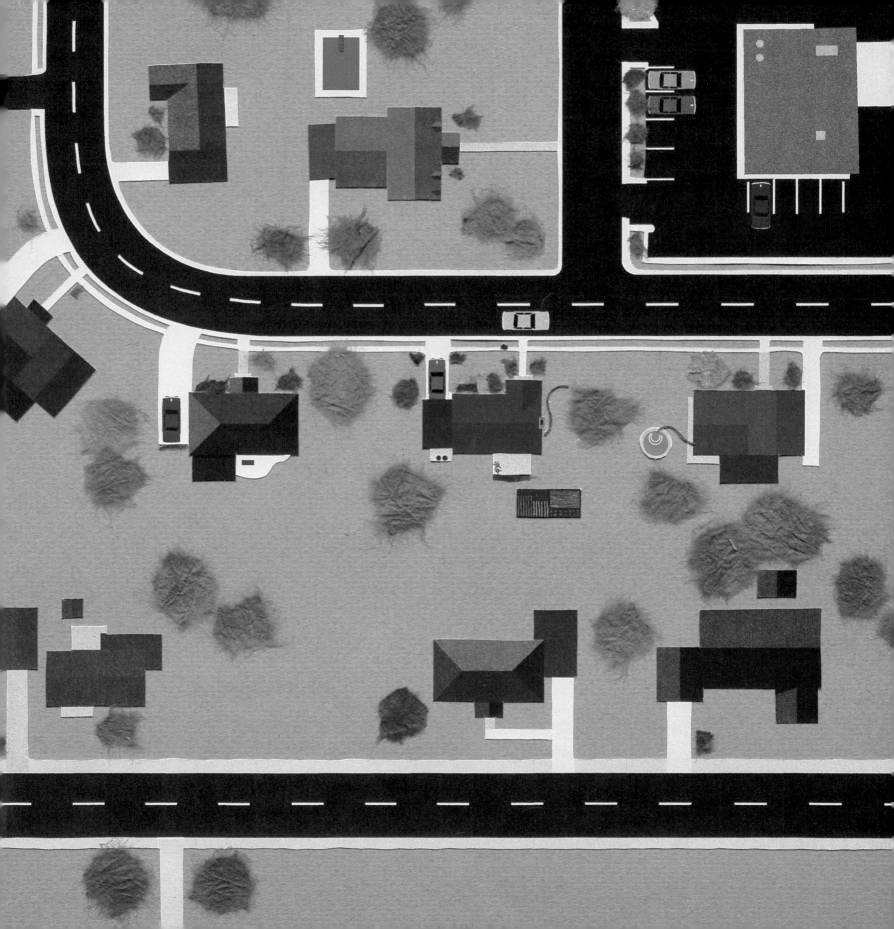

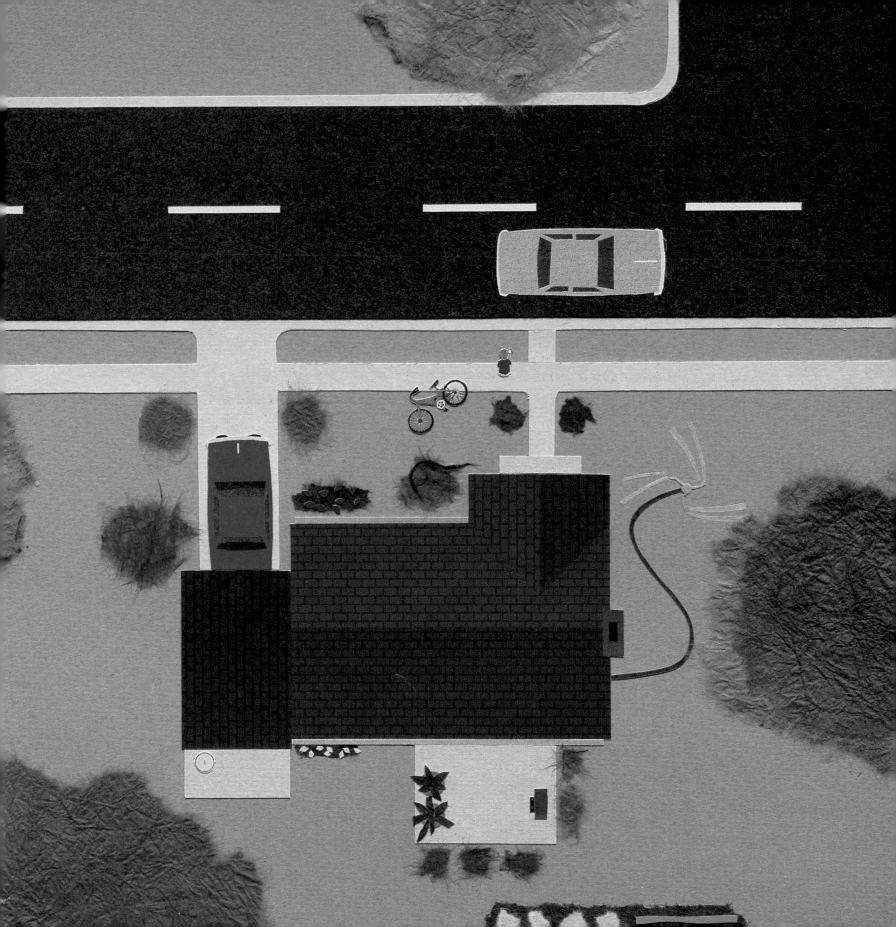

FOR MY MOTHER AND FATHER

The town we are "looking down" at in this book is not a real one, but it is like many towns on the East Coast of the United States between Maryland and South Carolina. In that part of the country, many farming communities have become big towns with more people and larger buildings.

www.houghtonmifflinbooks.com

Library of Congress Cataloging-in-Publication Data   Jenkins, Steve.   Looking down / by Steve Jenkins.   p.   cm.
Summary: A series of views of one landscape is seen from progressively lower vantage points, beginning in outer space and ending with a view of a ladybug as seen by a kneeling child.
RNF ISBN 0-395-72665-4   PAP ISBN 0-618-31098-3
[1. Visual perception—Fiction.]   I. Title.   PZ7.J41737Lo   1995   [E]—dc20   94-38720   CIP   AC